PRAISE FOR *THE CAREGIVER*

"How difficult it is to ennoble suffering, but the poems of Caroline Johnson halo the courage of the day-to-day struggle of caregiving, the giving as well as the receiving. I'd encourage anyone in these situations (and aren't we all sooner or later?) to look to these poems for strength and hope (and, yes, even humor) in the face of the approaching inevitable."

—WILLIAM GREENWAY, Professor Emeritus of English, Youngstown State University. Author of *Selected Poems*, winner of the 2014 FutureCycle Press Poetry Book of the Year Award

"*The Caregiver*, while deeply personal, reflects the universal wonder of love, responsibility, remembrance and loss. It is deeply moving and I found myself pulled into the poet's life as I remembered mine. Thank you for the journey."

—ROSEMARIE COHEN, Grief Counselor, Adventist St.Thomas Hospice

"It is hard to find positives in a terrible disease like neurodegeneration, when it has no treatment or cure. Caregivers often suffer as much as the patient. Caroline Johnson turns her experiences as a caregiver into moving poetry filled with keen observations, humor, and hope. Her work gives us all an eloquent and inspiring expression of the triumph of hope in the face of the depredations of incurable disease. Her poetry rises to the highest standards of literature and puts into perspective our quotidian struggles with life's ordinary challenges."

—DR. ALEX KLEIN, Vice President Scientific Affairs, CurePSP

T0155092

THE
CARE
GIVER

POEMS BY
CAROLINE JOHNSON

Holy Cow! Press
Duluth, Minnesota
2018

Author photograph by Bill Johnson.

Book and cover design by Anton Khodakovsky.
Printed and bound in the United States of America.
First printing, Spring, 2018

ISBN 978-09986010-3-8
10 9 8 7 6 5 4 3 2

Holy Cow! Press projects are funded in part by grant awards from the Ben and Jeanne Overman Charitable Trust, the Elmer L. and Eleanor J. Andersen Foundation, the Cy and Paula DeCosse Fund of The Minneapolis Foundation, the Lenfestey Family Foundation, and by gifts from generous individual donors.

Holy Cow! Press books are distributed to the trade by Consortium Book Sales & Distribution, c/o Ingram Publisher Services, Inc., 210 American Drive, Jackson, TN 38301.

For inquiries, please write to: HOLY COW! PRESS,
Post Office Box 3170, Mount Royal Station, Duluth, MN 55803.
Visit *www.holycowpress.org*

for Mother, Father, and Donna—
and to all caregivers who support, nurture
and advocate for their loved ones.

CONTENTS

FOREWORD

IT'S HARD TO BELIEVE I spent twelve plus years of my life managing my parents' illnesses in all their Technicolor array. I put countless miles on my car, visited every weekend and more, got docked pay often when one of them was hospitalized, drove them to numerous doctor appointments, and the list continues. This does not even touch on the emotional exhaustion that goes with caregiving. "Managing" means talking to doctors, nurses, social workers, Certified Nursing Assistants (CNAs), physical and occupational therapists, speech pathologists and other healthcare professionals. At each bump in the road there are always decisions to make: Do we choose home health care? Should we hire a CNA or a caregiver? What about a nursing home? As their Healthcare Power of Attorney, I felt the full responsibility of being their advocate. I prayed I made the right choices.

I came to write the poems in this book as a way to grapple with all of the unknowns of terminal illness, and to search for meaning as I witnessed my parents struggle. I had no precedent. I never planned to be a family caregiver. The job was thrust on me.

It began when my mother could never remember her lines in a play she was acting in, and my father had a shooting pain down his right leg. Mom later would wear her pajamas the whole day. These precursors morphed into full-blown Alzheimer's, Hydrocephalus and Rheumatoid Arthritis for my mother, and Parkinson's for my father (though later he was rediagnosed with a more rare neurological disease, Multiple System Atrophy). My father had acted as caregiver to my mother until we saw the negative effects on him, so we decided to hire a caregiver. Thank God for Donna, who provided the tender loving care both of my parents so desperately needed, and who taught me what it means to care for another beyond all thoughts of myself.

Some of these poems began at my parents' house and were inspired by films I watched with them, such as *The Titanic* ("Sunsets"), *300* ("This Old Soldier"), and many James Bond and Charlie Chaplin movies ("James"; "A Father's Invitation"). Others were written far away, such as "Shapeshifting" and "Eating Lobster" when I was on vacation with my husband, "At the Dentist" when I was getting a root canal, and "Flying" while en route to Europe. These poems reveal that caregiving stays with you always, and never leaves your mind or heart.

My father was a bomber pilot in the Air Force during the Cold War, hence I wrote poems that referenced this: "Parkinson's Flight," "Gliding," "Hospice," and "The Window." I didn't know him during that part of his life, but I can only imagine the courage it takes to fly a plane, perhaps the same courage it takes to tackle a life-threatening illness.

The title poem, "The Caregiver," was inspired after reading a Philip Levine poem about a worker on an assembly line. I couldn't help but think of what Donna did for my parents every day. Other poems, such as "A Good Day," "MSA," "Skiing," and "Glasses" attempt to show how stalwart my parents were in the face of chronic illness, while "Alzheimer's Dream," "Three Words," and "The Longest Good-Bye" touch on the defeat I often felt as caregiver, watching helplessly from the sidelines.

You may notice some of the poems in this book include animals. I frequently bicycle at a nearby nature canal and see herons, turtles, coyote, and deer. Some of these animals have made their way into my poetry, such as "Coyote" and "Changing Lanes," both about my mother. I have always associated turtles with my father. One of his favorite sayings was, "Be like a turtle. Let your problems roll off your back." Every time I see turtles while bicycling I still think of him (hence the poem "Crossing"). I wrote "Ode to My Father's Nursing Home" during a week-long seminar in 2016 with poet Natalie Diaz in Bemidji, MN. Somehow, turtles figured prominently in that poem. My father lived only two months in the nursing home. Do I regret we moved him? You bet, as it involved the constant policing of staff. But I tried to make its sterile existence palatable by bringing him homemade beet soup and listening to books on CD with him, such as *20,000 Leagues Under the Sea*, all of which inspired the poem, "Exile."

Finally, there is the whole element of grief, because in truth as caregiver you are grieving the entire time you see your loved one decline. Many of my poems touch on this, such as "Bones" where I could not get the line *I'm living far from the bone* out of my head, or "The Window," where I witnessed my father countless times attempting to get out of his hospital bed. I wrote "*Der Schrei*" at 3 a.m. in one sitting, with Allen Ginsberg's "Howl" in front of me. "Awake in the Woods" and "The Gallery" were written about my mother after her death.

It is an intimate bond, the caregiving relationship. From making sure your parents are clean and comfortable, to constantly talking to doctors and nurses about their care, it is definitely a responsibility. When you listen to your mother repeating the same stories over and over as you experience the strangeness of her not really knowing who she is, this teaches you patience. Feeding your father homemade oatmeal, scrambled eggs, and thickened drink becomes a spiritual act. I have found that a lot of other people also share these stories. Whenever I read my poems in front of people it sparks a reaction in them. Many times strangers come up to me after readings and tell me their caregiving stories. I also had the opportunity to read some of the poems to my father at the end of his life, and though I have no idea how much he comprehended, he seemed very appreciative. At his funeral in November of 2015, I read some poems instead of a eulogy.

I have no children, just a husband and two cats. The role of family caregiver was a natural one for me as all my siblings have kids, and some live far away from Chicago. I have worked as a newspaper reporter, barista, English teacher, office clerk, secretary, and now college advisor. I didn't grow up saying, "I would like to be a caregiver." But I have found caregiving to be the most important, profound job I've ever had. It has been a privilege and an honor to be by my parents' side during their later years. I experienced moments, like when my mother gave me one of her prized acrylic paintings she created, or when my father told me he "appreciated what I was doing" when Donna and I got him into a reclining wheelchair so he could see the sunset. This, of course, towards the later part of his illness. There were also many car rides home with the inevitable watery eyes.

As an advocate for my parents, I got the chance to help and understand them in a way most people can't. Though it was my job to speak for them when they couldn't speak for themselves, the most important (and often most challenging) thing was to remember they were going through a much more difficult rite of passage than I was. And though I still mourn the loss of them, I honestly wouldn't change the experience for anything. Caregiving forces you to consider the age-old struggle of letting go vs. hanging on. It constantly makes you wonder if you did enough. And though it is certainly not an easy task, caregiving changes you, makes you more human. We all need more of that.

Caroline Johnson
October 15, 2017

Sunsets

The sun has not set on the golf course.
We are watching *The Titanic* at home.
Kate Winslet has almost thrown herself
into the Atlantic's icy waters.
I like Kate Winslet.
She is pretty and a mother.
I am tall and I am not a mother.
My dad reaches over his wheelchair, fumbling
for the remote. "What are you doing, Dad?"
He says he's looking for his glasses, another
thing for me "to bitch about."

Mom thinks Kate Winslet is her mother.
Mom thinks this is not her house.
Mom is happy in her delirium.
"Are you OK, Bob?" she asks. "I love you."

I give my father his electric toothbrush and assist
him to the toilet. I cook them frozen pizza and clean
after them. I wonder if they will be in a nursing
home. "I'll be in there someday," my dad says.

The Titanic is sinking. Leonardo DiCaprio is trying
to save Kate Winslet. I like Leonardo DiCaprio.
At this moment, I do not like my father.
At this moment, I hope things will change.

Leonardo DiCaprio's lips are turning blue. My mother's
arms are scaly and dry. I put lotion on her arms.
I put lotion that smells like coffee on my father's legs,
bright with red sores. I tuck them into bed
and spread the fat green comforter over them.
Mom leans up with her dentureless mouth and smiles
a wide beam. "Thank you for being so nice," she says.
I kiss them on the cheek. My father says good-bye
and looks up with a blank stare, grabbing the comforter.

I go out to my black Honda. The sun is setting on the golf course.
All the golfers are finished, and there is only the red flag
blowing on the 18th hole, like a ghost.

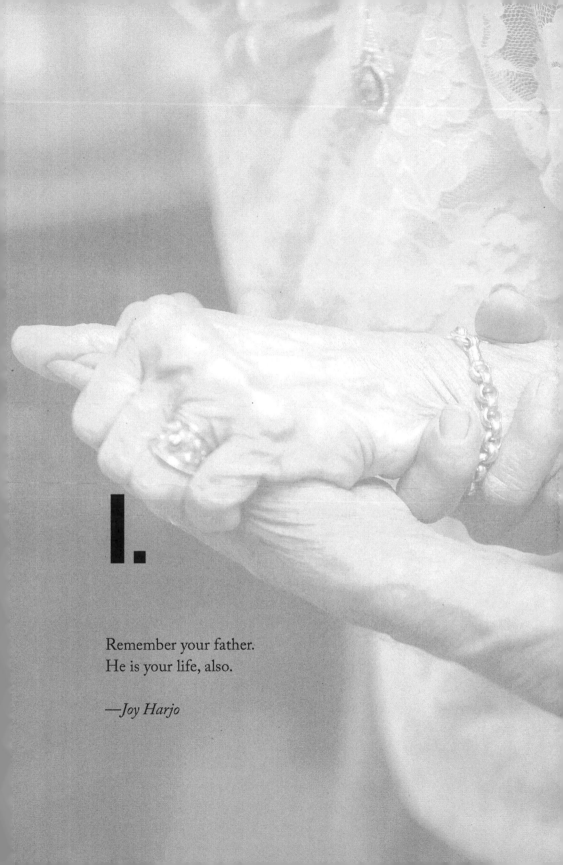

I.

Remember your father.
He is your life, also.

—*Joy Harjo*

CROSSING

Today I came across a painted turtle
as I was bicycling near a canal.

He had stopped in the middle of the trail,
head erect, all limbs exposed, waiting.

He seemed stuck in the moment,
moving neither forward nor backward,
trapped in time.

I thought of you, dear father,
moving across unstable ground,
gripping your cane and hovering
for a brief moment

before the storms set in.

Life's Melody

"I have found if you love life, life will love you back."
—Arthur Rubenstein

I had a dream my father stood up, walked
out of his wheelchair into transience,
into life, into that vast Design like the patient
spider who spins silk ribbons as we listen
to Chopin's nocturnes. And how did you
play them, Arthur? Did you not merge
with the music and disappear into the Divine?
And isn't it time, Father, for all of us
to slip into our own surreal world,
which remains lost until we stand
up, push aside our chair, and reclaim it?

SHAPESHIFTING

We are walking on the oldest rock in the world.
Basalt. It's part of the Canadian Shield, you said.
Striated black basalt formed from hot lava four billion
years ago, later tilting and shifting to the surface.
I hold your hand as we climb over wet stone
and migrate through sand. A bird sings
as the sun sizzles into Lake Superior. Earlier
we saw four snapping turtles laying eggs.
Golden waves spin a quilt of gossamer threads
as we sit on ancient rock and watch the sunset.
You tell me the L.A. Kings and the Devils are tied
in the Stanley Cup playoffs. I hold some rocks
in my hand—preserved, not fossilized. One
a perfect oval, one a trapezoid, another a hooded
figure, a wise shaman hovering over a drum,
or a Ku Klux Klan member carrying a stick.
Or perhaps it is an Indian chief bearing
robes and head dress, or maybe even
my father in his hospital gown, bending
down to pick up lost golf balls.

BECOMING ERUDITE

Long ago you told me your father
tried to hypnotize all four of his sons.
You didn't remember much, except
you wanted to be smarter, and afterwards
you immediately began reading the dictionary
page by page, while your brothers laughed.

When it was trendy in the 1970s, you
sat us down one by one. I counted
slowly to one hundred. You told me
to close my eyes, but I remember
peeking at a blinking Christmas light.
Your voice was smooth, intoxicating,
like the vodka tonic on the side table.
We sat together for 10 or 15 minutes,
you feeling more confident despite
each sip, me drunk on the attention.

Now I spend quiet afternoons with you
in your wheelchair. The voices of Dan Rather
and Wolf Blitzer hypnotize us. Now and then
you close your eyes and I speak to you
in hushed tones, coffee in hand. You worry
about your finances as you grip the remote,
the panic of losing control aching into
each hour, each minute, each second.

Your Last Chance

Out of the warm respite of cradling arms,
of childhood's easy embrace,
down the corridor of doctor's distant glow,
where worn leather black bag reveals
tools of experience and years of practice,
where each wrinkle shows smiles of promise,
and yesterday's dreams drum out a heartbeat
of EKGs and good-byes, where laughing soaks your eyes,
and each handshake and kiss is a blue mosaic to aching—
your dreams fall back, your memories are what's left,
the blackjack table now lies waiting as you
watch the dealer collect your folded hand.
You're not pretending anymore, your chips are low.
You've reached the Velveteen Rabbit's goal—
the moment of realness now is present as you
watch the sleek silver Santa Fe go barreling by,
the track all rusted, your last chance to hop
on the caboose and spring forward into the game.

Dangerous Driving

"The car is a lethal weapon," my father swore
to me when I was getting my driver's license.

Still I went on, laughing at him, driving to the most
dangerous places, pushing the accelerator
as fast and hard as I could.

I received my stack of speeding tickets,
and my father threatened to remove
my name from the insurance policy.

"The car is a lethal weapon," he said again.

Thirty years later, my brakes go out while
driving on a busy Chicago expressway.
I read the billboards, numb, unable to stop.

I get my car fixed, then we take the keys
away from my father, who is struggling
from years of Parkinson's disease.

"The car is a lethal weapon," I tell him,
but he still wants to drive.

JAMES

Bond is in bed with a
negligee-clad cat woman.

I ask one question:
"I thought he always got the girl.
The *good* girl," I add.

"Not *always*," Dad says softly
in a throaty voice, gently
emphasizing the *always*.

A Father's Invitation: A Sestina

He sips slowly from his glass of red wine.
We talk and laugh, looking at the TV.
I tell him about my day and he listens to me.
"You can come over any time," he says.
In the background we hear the news,
and we both agree the weather is fine.

Two months later, he says he feels fine
despite walking with a shuffle. The wine
sits on the table as we watch Chicago news
and the latest crime. Then he turns off the TV.
"The doctor ordered a walker," he says.
His hand shakes as he tells this to me.

Six months pass, and it's difficult for me.
I am depressed, but say on the phone I am fine.
"You can come over any time," Dad says.
"It will be fun. We'll drink a glass of wine."
He can't chew well. Still, he watches TV,
and we both try not to think about the news.

"So I need a wheelchair," he breaks the news
a year later as he turns away from me.
We hear Wolf Blitzer preaching on the TV
about the election and all the fine
candidates. I think about wine.
"Let's listen to some music," he says.

My boyfriend breaks up with me and says
he has to leave. I cry softly at the news,
then open another bottle of wine.
I call my father and he tells me,
"Come over. I know you'll be fine.
We'll watch Charlie Chaplin on TV."

Years later, as we peer out at the TV,
he nods from his hospital bed and says,
"Sean Connery is my favorite Bond, a fine
actor." I ask if he wants to hear any news,
but he shakes his gaunt head and asks me
if he could just have a glass of wine.

We drink grape juice wine and he tells me
nothing's new. The TV drones on. He says
still, "Come again anytime. We'll be fine."

AT THE DENTIST

The dentist was drilling and drilling
'til he reached the dead nerve of my tooth.
All I could see was a blinding light
and I thought, as the dental assistant sprayed
my gums with one more round of water,
there goes another molar,
and I thought, as I looked at the television
with Rachel Ray cutting up mushrooms,
we are all souls, connecting bone to blood,
and I remembered when my father used to make
marinated mushrooms, and I leaned back
into the reclining chair, the smell of mouthwash
and fluoride as I sucked on the vacuum.
The dental assistant asked me another question
I couldn't answer, my mouth full,
the dentist kept drilling and probing
'til I thought there was nothing left.
And Rachel Ray was beginning to boil
fat pasta and sauté the mushrooms,
and I remembered how my father told
me last month he was making marinated
mushrooms, how faint yet full of joy
his demented voice sounded
as he invited me to feast with him.
And I told him I loved marinated
mushrooms. "Then they'll be for you
and me," he said from his hospital bed.
"Come over any time." But I don't want
to talk about marinated mushrooms.

I want to write about the skinny
boy who drove me in the funny white van
decorated with red, green and blue circles,
to the dealer, and how he told me
they don't make Honda cars like
they used to. "The hard part is done,"
the dentist was saying, pushing the light
away from my head. I touched my tooth
with my tongue, tasted blood, and went
to pay my bill.

BONES

When I wander away from love
only horror haunts my nights.
I am living far from the bone.
I try hard not to wail or weep,
but grief gathers in my lap
like a forgotten kitten, white
noise and garbage intrude
on my silence. I wake in the night
counting the people who did me
wrong, sink into the black hole
of my pillow, shiver and soak up
TV violence, begin to lie to everyone,
forget how to laugh and kiss.

When I find myself murmuring
to a Macy's sales clerk something
about my father's rare neurological
disorder, his one crossed eye,
his jaundice and joy at my voice,
it is then I am closer to the bone.
I go outside to find Orion, trace
each constellation with my finger,
draw a celestial skeleton across
the sky, offer up an incantation
to the gods of night.

When I find myself on the doorstep
of my father's house, cross the threshold
and enter his room, say hello and kiss
his cheek—when he greets me from his
hospital bed—here, I am not cold anymore
as I feed him spoonsful of applesauce,
ask him about the stars, then cover
his ancient bones with a handmade quilt.

FLYING

Taxiing down the runway—a man
leans over his seat—hushes two girls
in full-length black burkas—nearby
identical twin girls—separated
by the aisle—listen to the same music.

High powered jets—slow to take off—
full throttle—loud—thundering—
the hot rod of the cloud highway—
then no wheels—unbearable air—
not even your voice—just glide.

I settle in my seat—think of Dad
in his wheelchair—we will all be sitting
the next seven hours—like Dad sits,
always sitting, sitting, looking, sleeping—
I close my eyes. Only 3,944 miles to go.

Parkinson's Flight

Such a long way to go
and the driver looks tired,
big engine jet, shiny, not new,
gassed up for flight in a crowded sky.

You used to fly solo
with a bomb in the back,
never gave out directions,
never cracked under attack.
You look out the window,
a passenger now,
thunder sound in the distance,
plane turns to take off
all eyes look up and pray.

You close the book
you've been reading
and look straight ahead,
not dreaming but reminiscing,
a former pilot now resting,
a veteran in flight
on a jumbo 747 to Denver.

Yet just a while ago
gray eyelashes stuck, feet stumbling,
body drifting in the bushes from a fall.
Hand gnashed, skin torn,
a bandage to cover the damage.
Buttonholes fumbled, shoestrings tangled,
zippers now a struggle, hand tremoring
to an unpunctuated gate.

Now everything is like throwing a snowball
on a well-lit fire. The ashes of your youth
lie scattered. Your pride kindles sharply,
melting under stress—you chew slowly
because the pilot is tired, yet

still determined in resolution,
still awake in constitution,
you bow your head, giving forth
light from within.

The flight attendant passes by
touches your shoulder with a sigh
and asks, "Are you all right, sir?"

Gyrating and with a stoned face,
you nod—a smoky, shaky dream—
a hero on a wheelchair team,
entering another cockpit world
you salute your Captain with solemn
grace, accepting all that is your fate.

GLIDING

"What am I but a solitary gull between earth and heaven?"
—*Tu Fu*

I don't fear black holes.
Everyone has one, a dark star.
When you pass into it, gravity
bends—your feet pull, your head
stretches. But for now, warm

thermals push you and me over
farms and lakes. A ridge of wind lifts
us into the ether. With no engine,
carried only by waves of energy,
we glide in a tandem cockpit.

So many years ago you told me
your theory about death.
You called it the *black hole theory*.
We all disappear, you said.
That's all. Nothing. Nada.

You dolphin down away from
darkness. A seagull arches
over water, his wings stretched
to get the most wind. He glides.
We glide. It is all about lift, you say.

We soar at an even ratio, our glider
sifting through the silence of the clouds.
Father, you can stay airborne for hours
by piloting us through the rising air.
Only sun and shadows here.

Yet I know it's going to end.
You are going to die, I am going
to die. We will vacate these bodies,
this planet, disappear into that frozen
star you speak of. No energy.

No light. Just decayed matter
500 billion years old. But what
happens to the light, I wonder.
Will we fall like Icarus, our faith
a cruel joke? Or will we rebound,

jump back like a kite billowing on
cyclones and velocity? Father, stay
airborne. Stay part of the Milky Way.
Don't leave me. Keep drifting,
for what are we but gulls gliding?

The Window

You close your eyes, body curled up
in a hospital bed. You lean your life

against a pillow, talk to imaginary
friends, eat the air, wrestle with angels,

breathe canisters of manufactured
oxygen, swallow a pink pill.

On the dresser sits a black and white
photo of you in uniform, antique radio

gear attached to your head, dark hair
neatly combed back. You are smiling.

I ask about religion, and you tell me
about a bay window full of stars that leads

to a galaxy of black holes, light years
from where we are here. I look out

your bedroom window, framed by
a handmade flower curtain, searching

for your soul full of light that could
frame your face, free it of fear.

All I see are perfect black mailboxes
propped in front of fabricated houses.

Now and then you throw your legs
over the guard rails, trying to escape

from an unchosen life as you sink
into your pressure sensitive mattress.

You shout, "Close the window!" and
as I draw the shade I see Charon ferry

his passengers across Styx, towards
Lethe and the tall reeds of forgetting.

FEEDING YOURSELF

Your needle-pricked hand fingers
your face, touches your curly eyelashes
as the IV machine clicks, the blood
pressure monitor hums. I shove

a fork into your hand and announce,
"Dinner time!" You attempt to stab
the overcooked broccoli but fail,
your fork not positioned correctly.

You try again, this time with stuffing.
Still no luck, but you bring the empty fork
up to your mouth anyway. I take
the utensil out of your hand, scoop

up the supper, then cue you to open
your mouth. You eat, obediently.
You finish your dinner, every bite.
I lay down the fork. Your hand moves

gracefully towards the plate, grasping
at the empty hospital tray, then up again
to your mouth. The movement is repetitive,
as you shovel the imaginary food to your

open mouth and take a nibble of empty air.
Down and up, you raise and lower your hand,
grasping, pretending to feed yourself. You
can't stop. You are not pretending.

I push the tray away and open your high school
yearbook. I point to the faces, and you recite
each of the fifty names by heart. You even whisper
who was a cheerleader, who the chess champ.

I read to you a signature: "To Bob, a swell guy."
You give a wry smile and nod your head.

THE CAREGIVER

See this Lithuanian woman. She has been
feeding my father dinners of mashed turkey
and broccoli, potato pancakes, washing his
clothes, bathing him, offering him the choice
between Wolf Blitzer and Vanna White for years.

Observe her hands as they gently push his body
to the side of the hospital bed. They are covered
with latex gloves. Consider the way she has taught
me to tenderly pull up his socks and cover him
with a quilt, put drops in his eyes, rub powder
on a rash, splash his neck with Old Spice, then
bend down to kiss his cheek goodnight.

You must come closer, you must hang up your jacket,
be prepared to spend hours listening to his slurred
speech, help feed him applesauce with vitamins,
raise and lower his bed, monitor his erratic heartbeat.
Remember what he has given up—his Buick LeSabre,
his cane, his walker, then finally his wheelchair—to get
to where he now lives, a bed with guard rails.

Go to the night-stand and offer him a Frango Mint.
Put on his favorite Garrison Keillor CD. Listen as he
smiles with his one good eye and whispers something
so faint, you ask him to repeat, "I'm lucky."
Think about all this while driving the long way home.

You may get angry at the world, like I do, until you
see your husband asleep in the Lazy-Boy, bare legs
dangling. Until you suddenly realize what the caregiver
has taught you as, without a word, you slowly rub lotion
onto your husband's chapped heels, then cover his ice-cold feet.

A Good Day

He was having a good day. A nurse evaluated him. He couldn't answer most questions, but he knew it was spring. He couldn't sign his name. He thought it was January. Still, he was having a good day.

I wanted to leave. I had done my time—spent hours with the nurse and his caregiver. I had to grade papers, buy some groceries, get home to have dinner with my husband. But he was having a good day, and when I tried to say good-bye, he asked when he would see me again. I told him soon, and that I would bring cake.

"Cake?" he asked, expectantly. I asked him what kind he would like. "Chocolate," he said from his hospital bed.

So I left and went to Jewel, then returned with two giant pieces of cake. Red velvet with cream cheese frosting, and marble cake frosted with chocolate. He chose the red velvet.

I spoon fed the red velvet cake into his mouth. He said it was very good. Afterwards, I turned on CNN and stayed to chat. He played with my key chain like an infant. He reached up and tried to unzip my sweatshirt. He pointed to my T-shirt.

"It's *The Scream*," I said. "A painting by Edvard Munch."

He smiled and reached out to touch me. He said one word.

"What did you say, Dad?" I asked.

"Heart," he whispered, then closed his eyes.

THE LAST BED

—on viewing Abraham Lincoln's death bed, Chicago History Museum

It's king-sized, fit for any large man,
except perhaps our slain president.
At six feet four inches, he fit only diagonally
across the mattress at Petersen's Boarding House.

The blood probably seeped into the black
and gold spread and ivory sheets.
The twisted black cherry oak frame
supported his battle-weary body
as Mary held his hand until 7:23 a.m.
when his last breath came.

And now I see you, Father, lying
in your hospital bed, the silver railings,
the pressure sensitive mattress, the electric
motor that lifts your head up and down.

And who will deliver your Emancipation
Proclamation? Will I be holding your cold,
frail hand when you decide to leave this land?

MSA*

It's the turning into the forest, a letting
go of gold leaves as they fall silently onto
the quilt of reds, browns, and greens sewn
into the autumn hillside. Perhaps the hardest

thing is slowing down, to remember we
can't make leaves stay as they drift away,
one by one, from bleached branches
crowded with sleepy cormorants.

It's the tearing away from embrace,
the arms that once held so tight, the smile
sinking into the hospice pillow, ashes
on your swollen face, the way waxy

pale thin skin breaks into blisters,
covering cold skeleton, and blood so tired
from the flood of soft food as you summon
energy for another fight, resting, waif-like,

a broken kite in a hospital bed. It's the
slurred speech, the slow grin of gargoyles
dancing into the grotesque, the cry of ravens
slowly marching into divine slumber.

---

* *MSA is an acronym for Multiple System Atrophy, a neurological disorder similar to Parkinson's*

Hospice

When you watch someone die
you must sit up close and open
your heart to pronounce each vowel,
you must let your loved one
embrace the air, let his arm
extend towards infinity,
you must help him
touch the stars.

When you watch your father die
remember it is a privilege
to stroke his stone cheek,
to kiss his forehead,
to tuck his hair behind his ears.
You must try not to be
so important, you must wave
when he decides to leave.

When you watch a bomber pilot die
who once got lost in the threshold
of a dream, remember he no longer
needs his walker, his cane, his wheelchair,
remember there will come a day
when he will no longer need you
will no longer need his body
though you will pray for him

to bring back the light as he flies
past one thousand sunrises in the sky.

II.

The most beautiful word on the lips of mankind
is the word "Mother."

—*Kahlil Gibran*

SHUT-INS

It is snowing softly. Mother grips
the steering wheel with gloved hands,
intent on our mission. She turns down

a tree-lined street and slowly pulls
up to a darkly-lit house with peeling
gray paint, sagging porch, so different

from the other Victorian houses with
perfect trim and lighted driveways.
I can smell the pine from the back

of our Buick, where a dozen wreaths
fill the seats, each tied with a homemade
red ribbon. "Here," she says, thrusting

a large one into my small hands.
"Go up there and ring the doorbell."
Numb, I blink and feel I am at the dentist

after the pricking of Novocain and a dull
toothache. "Go on," she says, pushing me
out the door. So I walk, my legs weak,

frozen, clutching the wreath tightly,
into the dark night and towards Mrs. Smith,
my first lesson in kindness.

Triptych in Color

—*after viewing James McNeil Whistler's "Arrangement in Gray and Black No. 1," Art Institute of Chicago*

I

Whistler painted his mother with thin paint, black on gray,
a tulle bonnet framing her stern, stoic face. She clutches
a frilled handkerchief, looks tired though she is seated.
Her gigantic ebony gown covers everything but her Puritan
feet, which rest on a wooden box. Perhaps it was the Sabbath.
Did anyone bring her flowers? Did she ever smile?

II

If I painted my mother, it would be all color. A yellow sundress,
fresh cut daffodils, blonde hair and a Marilyn Monroe smile.
Perhaps she would be seated around a table painting ceramics,
which is what she liked to do when she wasn't hosting parties.
On another canvas, she holds the hand of my dying sister.
What you can't see is our upright Kimball. What you can't hear
are the fragile melodies my sister used to play, the way I
performed the same songs years later at my parents' dinner
parties, my mother humming along and swaying her body.

III

I can imagine Whistler's mother and my own sitting together.
Whistler would be in the next room, painting his new masterpiece.
Then they would ask me to play. I'm no artist, but the relief
of putting fingers to black and white keys carries me to a softer
time, when I was younger and holding my mother's hand.

Coyote

To Mother, May 19, 2006

I saw a coyote the other day
walking across a busy four-lane highway.
Unnerved by the traffic, he took his time
and slowly ambled into the woods.
You are like that coyote now—strong, free
and healthy—conquering all fears and
blissful of your surroundings. You have
crossed the road of troubles, and emerged
to return into the forest of your life—
not frail and afraid, like the deer,
not nervous and skittish, like the squirrel,
not a scavenger, like the raccoon,
but awesome and upright, harboring a
deep purpose and an elevated spirit,
a soul that has conquered misfortune,
and a camouflaged will to travel on.

SKIING

My mother skies like an Olympian,
diving down moguls of locked memories,
navigating knee replacements and broken bones.

When she fears she might hit a tree,
she makes angels in the powder, dodges
chronic arthritis with pain pills and lightning.

In the warming hut of her kitchen, she works
on jigsaw puzzles of kittens and blue sky while
sipping hot chocolate and nibbling donut holes.

Her shirt is red checked like the wallpaper
in her kitchen, and when she zips down each slope,
out of bounds, her hand-knit scarf tied

in an unreadable knot, she becomes a blur,
a French Impressionist dancer with a couple
of pieces missing, a potpourri, a broken mirror.

She stands up from her wheelchair clutching her cane—
a monogrammed rod, a wooden crutch, a tree branch,
an extended piece of willow, a bleached crow—

then plants it like a pole, attempting to descend
the stairs one more time, each icy step a flag of victory,
a fast blue slope, a thrilling dangerous carousel ride.

She carves her boots into the carpet like orthopedic
ornaments, slowly slides her patella, joints and femur,
her titanium knees, her aching shoulders, summoning

her courage, then points her skis towards the bottom
of the mountain—where the powder and ice await,
where we all will be someday—closes her eyes, and lets go.

PAIN

At 6:30 p.m., the pain came.
        She pricked like a spent balloon in the sky.
        Puckered, a bald swan, she began to fly into the night,
Bruised.

Will she burst seeds and weep?
        Slide down your back, past arteries and spleen?
        Through your knees, joints, into your bony shoulders,
Unseen.

A pretty wolf, she howls
        plays acupuncture with your heart, pierces skin,
        prowls past midnight, stabs your song, drowns your
Sailboat.

Will she stay with you always like a battle wound,
        or will she leave you in some truck stop
        scarred with a silent bullet
Abandoned?

A lonely miner who hitchhikes her way
        across your skin, she turns and dives into your scars,
        keys your car, braids your hair, then
Disappears.

Eating Lobster

—on an Alaskan ship at sea

The Filipino waiter, Arnaldo, lifts my lobster
fresh flown from Maine onto another plate,
picks at it with two sharp knives,
removes it from its shell,
then cuts a prawn lengthwise.
He handles the seafood expertly
puts only the meat back onto my plate.

Dressed in his navy sailor suit,
a nautical tie and striped suit,
he looks comfortable at sea.

So many times I have cut Father's
food into tiny pieces so he could chew
easily with his Parkinson's, and Mother's,
too, so she could swallow slowly
despite her dentures and dementia.

I take several bites and realize I have
deposited food in my left cheek
like a chipmunk, like Mother does.
I am no longer hungry.

Glasses

Sitting in his wheelchair, Father struggles
to brush his teeth, sips from an antique
green glass hand blown by Grandpa,
spits into a pink plastic hospital tray.

Mother also rinses her mouth with one
of Grandpa's vintage juice glasses.
After polishing her dentures, she
wanders off to bed, her head full
of sweet, demented delusions.

Earlier we hunted for her lost
hearing aid, searched among socks,
drains, under dressers, beds, until we
found it buried deep in the bottom
of one of her father's speckled glasses.

I tuck them into bed, tell them about
a puffin I saw in Alaska. Mother
wonders when she will fly away.
"Is that where we're going?
she asks. "To Alaska?"

I can't argue with her logic,
merely dim the lights.

Who am I to tell her
she doesn't have wings?

Alzheimer's Dream

You're a stranger to me now,
though I've known you all my life.
So long ago I wandered into your kitchen
to inquire when dinner would be ready,
and if there were anything I could make.
You smiled instantaneously as you do now,
and I helped you peel potatoes, snap
green beans. But today you forgot me again
and the day and the occasion, but no matter,
we're making baked potatoes, green beans,
and steak, I think, to eat while we watch
the imaginary parade and fireworks—
an early Fourth of July.

Let's sit down here and talk.
Let's look at the weather.
Let's do everything to be together.
Let's try not to remember,
have a drink to forget
that we ever once met a lifetime ago
when I called you mother
and needed you so.

DONUT HOLES

They were not French beignets, though Mom would make those, too.

> *"Que sera, sera," she hums, setting the table for four.*
> *No one is coming to visit, but she is determined.*
> *Her eyes seem glazed, coated like a donut.*
> *"Bon Vivant! Ami, amor! I shall like some French bread!"*

They were not croissants, nor were they fancy napoleons.

> *"Do you know someone has given me a whole closet of clothes!*
> *Caroline, did you do that?" She struggles with the silverware.*
> *"Or was that the **other** Caroline?"*

My mother invented a breakfast pastry to compete with my father's male gourmet society.

> *"This is not my house. I must find my house!*
> *I am sure the other Caroline has kidnapped me!*
> *We have got to find my house!"*

She took an empty plastic medicine bottle, punched holes from biscuit dough, plopped them into grease, then coated them with cinnamon sugar.

> *My mother is a giant donut hole that has separated from its sticky surface.*
> *Her eyes, crater-like, look beyond the kitchen, a broken lightbulb goes off*
> *and she gives a delirious grin. "Nina," she speaks to her childhood dog.*
> *"You've come back!" She asks the air, "Mom? Where have you been?"*

Beads

It used to be a necklace
verdant green and milky blue orbs
small and medium globes
jade pendants with
intricate lines

now all spilled, broken
the string loosened
they are a collection
swiftly gathered
and put in a plastic bag

no longer interdependent,
a jangled group of precious
beads, mixed up, demented,
with no memory of how
they used to be.

No recollection of day
or night, now or then,
just beautiful beads,
the colors still dazzling,

no longer wearable, not showy,
yet still they shine—

like you.

WANDERING

—with a line borrowed from Joyce Carol Oates

You open the door and creak outside,
grabbing the frayed edges of your
pink flannel nightgown, stepping hesitantly
in stockinged feet, your legs scaly and dry,
your eyes open and wide.

Where are you going and where have you been?

"I'm going home," you say confidently, in a cloud
of delusion, as you step over yesterday's daffodils,
and walk away from the moon.

Your hair is tousled. The night air brushes your eyes.
Frazzled, curious, they are broken trees, twigs on fire,
now burnt shards. They peer out onto the surprise
of a familiar neighborhood that has changed—
a driveway cracked and splintered, houses
with brick siding, black mailboxes perfectly
propped like rows of coffins in blue moonlight.

Where are you going and where have you been?

Electrical energy explodes in the glow
like destroyed synapses. An airplane passes
above, the stars are fixed as you stumble
house to house, shying into each driveway.

"I'm going home," you say less confidently,
your smile a delirious holiday, your face pale
from the celestial light. You turn back and walk
inside to the house you have always known—
a palace called home, now strange and foreign.

Your caregiver locks the door. You finally take to sleep.
Your brain tired to the core, your body secret and sore.
While late into the night your family gathers to remember
how things used to be, when life was not a mystery.

Where are you going and where have you been?

Borders

"I'm so excited you're here!" she says,
joy in her voice, enthusiasm spreading
in her wide-open eyes
like an ocean of light.

Earlier, she stepped her seventy-six-year-old frame
across the threshold and onto the back deck.
She moved into transience, into the sunset
like the white egret across the lake.

"Will you take me home?" she asks,
not sure where she lives anymore,
not sure of her husband,
dementia clouding the sun

of her overactive mind. Still,
she wanders into each guest's memory,
making friends with strangers,
whistling a tune each day.

"I'm so glad you're here!" I say,
answering her momentum,
meeting her glorious spirit
as the egret slowly takes flight.

Taking Flight

Taking off
we speed down the runway
lights shimmer and fade
as we ascend into night.

Earlier I watched
a huge magenta sun
dip into the Minneapolis sky
as I dried my eyes.

Now the city lights
splinter the silence.
Fading away, we melt
into darkness, decay.

Just as your demented spirit
radiates from weary limbs,
spins skyward, sings hymns,
then descends.

A Mother's Love

She is sleeping, and if you listen
you can almost hear her breathe.
The nurse sits her up in bed.
She winks one eye open and I feed her
a spoonful of stuffing and gravy.
With brown eyes she smiles, and the
smile lasts me the whole day—
more than seventy-seven years,
more than one week in a hospital bed,
more than a generation,
more than the love a mother can show.

THREE WORDS

Just three words
shocked me
into submission,

moiled my heart,
wrapped their icy tentacles
across my veins,

sandbagged my joints
like arthritis,
pummeled my groin,
sparked me into a seizure.

Just three words
in the Emergency Room,
not the ones
I wanted to hear—
"I love you"

but instead
Do Not Resuscitate.

THE LONGEST GOOD-BYE

Yellow is her favorite color.
But now she is wearing
a white hospital gown,
needles in her veins, a tube
up her nose. She is breathing.

I am talking to a doctor on the phone.
She is talking about a nursing home,
about hospice care. She is talking about
Stage Three Alzheimer's, where patients
forget how to eat,
forget who they are.

It's been five months now
confined to a hospital bed,
now and then speaking gibberish,
now and then smiling.

I have to make a decision.
Where is my mother to go?

I look at the TV and see
a prairie of yellow wildflowers,
and I know.

Conjuring

I

Seeing mother as Raggedy Ann
in hospice clothes
shakes me up, rattles my bones.

Her coal black button eyes,
her faded red yarn hair,
her arms pale and wrinkled,
her gingham smile, now broken,

once connected people like bridges
over the Danube of Budapest.

I bend down to pick up a bleached log.
A halo of light pours on me,
spreading like a river of swans.

II

When the conference of birds sing their song,
I know she's made her peace and gone.

A lone southern belle who conjured friends
like fireflies, releasing them into the air,
she is now just a disheveled doll sailing
towards infinity and the atmosphere.

I dive into the oily water and swim,
but she has disappeared, a peasant
lost in a paprika field.

III

The swans have flown away, leaving only
a few white feathers on the river's surface.
The wind of her soul seeps through holes
in my log, creating a constant song.

III.

Grief is a river you wade in
    until you get to the other side.

—*Barbara Crooker*

What Got Him Here

What got my dad to be
a successful air force pilot,
accountant, father of four,
married for fifty-three golden years

until mother slipped away one day
with spastic breaths
and he was left alone
to roll along in his chair

still fighting for his right to drive
still fighting for his right to walk
and now—the last battle—
letting go of his finances

yet still he reaches for tax forms
and always asks if it's time to pay
the bills, if it's time to do taxes,
and I have to tell him

No, it is not time, now is not the time,
in fact it will never be the time.
When it snows or the sun shines,
there will be no taxes to complete.

What got him here?
Fumbling for the remote,
embraced by a nasty, cruel disease.
Where is his wife now?

Did she slip into the atmosphere
while the minister sang *a capella*
a hymn about going home?

And where is he going,
he wonders, as he stares
at Alex Trebek announcing
his next guest.

THIS OLD SOLDIER

I'm sitting in your wheelchair.
It is dusk.
We are watching the film, "300,"
about a bloody battle between
three hundred Spartan soldiers
and one million Persians.

I ask if it is okay to put a bronze
rose etched into pink granite
on your wife's grave.

King Leonidas helps his scant soldiers
build a wall around Thermopylae
to contain the numerous enemy.

"How does this work?" you ask,
fumbling for the remote.

Leonidas refuses the Persians' request
to lay down his weapons. You tell me
you want no cross on your grave.

Xerxes watches as his faithful
Persian soldiers are slaughtered
by a barrage of arrows.

I forget how hard it must be,
to fight for your life with all you've got
using the only weapons you have ever known
from this chair.

Changing Lanes

So now I'm driving home from a funeral, passing the yellow arches
of McDonald's, a 7-11, a forest preserve, a doe standing in the middle
of a frozen shipping canal. Bill says deer don't like ice. I like snow,
but I don't like black ice. Condensation is forming on my windshield.
I wipe it off and it smears. I think of my mother, blonde hair, pink lipstick
smeared, lilac dress in a rose casket. The undertaker asked if the
pearl earrings go with her. I don't care about the pearl earrings.
I do care about the tiny gold heart locket she is wearing because it has
a photo from my parents' wedding in 1958. Three of their grandchildren
perched around the casket, giggling and whispering. I guess they got tired
of playing Hide and Seek in the funeral home. Little Bobby dropped
a sealed letter to Grandma in her casket. I wonder what the letter says
as I see fingerprints where I smeared the glass. I think of my mother,
looking down from the sky with her pearl earrings shining like stars,
trying to touch us but leaving prints instead. Is death like that?
A game of Hide and Seek? My mom's heart is not tiny. I change lanes
and look again at the snow-covered canal, but I don't see the deer
anymore.

Memorium

Someone was saying*
something about sadness
the way darkness shrivels up your dreams,
gnarled like an oak tree
with CNN droning in the distance.

Someone whispered something
about a hot air balloon ride
the way I lean over
your hospital bed to feed you
another spoonful of applesauce.

Someone mentioned
how you once flew a B-47
with a nuclear bomb in the back,
as I move your hospital bed
up and down and bring to you
a model of the airplane.

Someone was telling me
to look at the moon
so I look at the hub of your crossed eye
and feel the eclipse of your
laughter, dancing in dark pupils.

Then your caregiver leans
into my ear, tells me to kiss you,
to tuck you in. So I put a vase
with one lone carnation next
to the photo of your wife.

---

* *With a first line from Mark Strand's poem, "From the Long Sad Party."*

A Widower's Wish

If from her casket bed she could rise,
and leave behind her body bruised and sore,
after months wasting in a slow demise,
her thin limbs shaken to the skeletal core.

If she could rise above her arthritic pain,
transcend time's cruel geometry unaware,
perhaps I could remember all over again,
and lift myself out of this wheelchair.

If she could rise, I say, if she could rise,
mix blood and spirit in the starry night.
Our twin souls would mingle like fireflies,
lifting skyward into the silver light.

I could greet my lover before death's abyss,
use alchemy to transform an eternal kiss.

REWIND

Undo a kiss
move backwards
disentangle yourself

pause stand up
turn left and walk
south towards the door

say good-night
to the evening sun
lace up your ice skates

move one foot
glide into night as if
your life depended

on it until you waltz
until you hug yourself
until you find where

you first were born
in the wrinkled arms
of your father's embrace

Navigare Vivere Est*

You, funeral of sails, I admit to you,
I am not born for this, this way
of leaving, this sad hospital stay
as when a ruby rash spreads
its infection ripe across your
jaundiced thigh. You open your
eyes after the twenty-second blood
test and sweet water flows through
your tired veins. Father, I admit
to you, I am not born for this,
this delusion creeping into
every kiss good-bye. Why not
let a slow smile bob across
your broken teeth and take
everyone in this lost hospital
room for a ride, you, funeral
of sails, once bearer of dry wit,
let us laugh again and open
the jib, then glide in the current
towards home.

---

* *Latin for "Sailing is Life." The poem's first two lines are taken from*
Aracelis Girmay's poem, "Jaconda."

ODE TO MY FATHER'S NURSING HOME

With its Lysol smell and hospital halls, this is not
the house he remembers. Patients in the memory
ward hug stuffed animals, ask you to give them a ride
in their motorized chairs, to take them home. The short,
dark-skinned nurse shakes her head, tells you they
can't check on your father every two hours:
We don't have the staff. He'll have to wait.
Your father, like a painted turtle, opens his eyes
and lifts his head. He is in a new terrarium,
his room full of photos and a model airplane,
cold tile floor like the river he escaped from,
his bed humming like crickets on a lily pad,
his pool of urine the eddy in a turtle's creek.
He cannot speak, is hoarse when he whispers,
cannot move quickly away from predators,
can only withdraw closer into his shell.
I feed him a spoonful of homemade beet soup.
A thick, milky tear trickles down his cheek
as I ask him if he knows where he is, and he
whispers, "Nooooo." A bed alarm continues
to go off down the hall. These turtles don't
want to play, they only want to escape their habitat,
tuck their limbs inside dark shells, and go home.

Exile

"The sea supplies all my wants...it is nothing but love and emotion."
—Captain Nemo

I am light years away except when I
think of you. Once I fed you homemade
beet soup, sweet and sour shrimp.
We watched *Shark Tank* and listened to
20,000 Leagues Under the Sea.
You thought you saw the photo
of Captain Nemo in your high
school yearbook. Meanwhile,

we orbited the sun. Men gathered
in their *polis*, worked to keep
the council fires burning, watched
as Hestia swept the hearth. Out
of deep darkness we were born,
drinking our days thirstily from
a generous cistern. But where

are you now? Lost in the underworld
ocean, or floating in an asteroid belt?
Have you felt the submarine's crash,
or the high voltage straight out of
Benjamin Franklin's kite? Can I
bring you butter pecan ice cream
again, wipe your blood red mouth,
a pomegranate juiced of seeds?

Once you were a prisoner in the Nautilus
of your nursing home, your only escape
the kindness of strangers. Captain Nemo
demanded loyalty even as your bone
and marrow slowly disappeared, even
when you departed to no man's land.

Inner stars burned as I watched
you take your last breath. I crawled
into a warm dark womb, gulped
my first lungful of salt water.

THE SNEEZE

For Father

I can still hear it
if I close my eyes

the shiver, the hesitation
before the pale muffled

explosion. You raise
your hand to shield

the spray. You may even
do it all over again, this

time hunching your shoulders
as if to deflect the blow.

Not like my husband, whose
cacophony crashes the ears

like a concert of cicadas
and who never uses a hankie

but turns his face towards
his armpit. No, you were

much more delicate, quiet,
your sneeze an airy thread

woven into a tapestry of moments
and I never noticed, never thought

I'd miss it, the way I miss you.

Awake in the Woods

There is light so I follow the gravel
road, turn left and walk into the woods.

Giant pine trees, soft ferns, a forest of friends
greet me. I think of you, and our last
good-bye when I was holding your cold,
wrinkled hand. Suddenly, I see blue
Forget-Me-Nots, then Yellow Lady Slippers
(your favorite color), and I turn a corner
only to hear the low throttle of the
Pileated Woodpecker. I move on,
overjoyed to see tiny ivory bells of
Lilly of the Valley, your favorite flower.

A purple moth darts from a bush.
I walk on, eager to see what is next.
In the dimpled light I see a giant black
bird, the Pileated, fly to another tree, its red
plumage prominently marked. I stop,
look again, but it is gone. I clip
two lilac blooms, also your favorite.

It is late afternoon, and I am awake,
awake in the woods, filled with Nature's
surprises and the soft light of your spirit.
Next time, I would need no map.

The Gallery

—at an art gallery outside Lutsen, Minnesota

For Mother

I walk alone into the small, isolated gallery.
Soothing music plays as I open the cabin door.

Paintings of waterfalls, loons, birches, clouds,
and mist rising from Lake Superior whisper
to me from the walls. They remind me of your oils:
midnight blue moons, burning orange leaves,
still lives of sunflowers, red poppies.

I read calligraphy cards and feel the comfort
of your spirit. ***I will wait for you,*** a card says.
In an empty field.

I know from this moment on that I am not alone.
If I do not go looking for you, but am open,
you will find me in the most unexpected places.

You will find me in the dialogue of my students,
in the cry of my neighbor's baby,
in the wisp of a dandelion seed.

DER SCHREI *

—for Mother and Father (after Allen Ginsberg)

I

I saw the best minds of my parents' generation destroyed by long,
    lingering disease, bodies torn by knee replacements, gout, crippling
    neurological ailments, rheumatoid arthritis,
who fought valiantly against urinary tract infections and shingles
who left home so many times because they forgot where they were
    and who they were
who lay in soiled diapers patiently waiting for someone to change them
who never complained about boiled broccoli or mashed potatoes
whose suppositories worked only sometimes
who woke in the night crawling, kicking, screaming, only to be pacified
    by Xanax and cranberry juice
who gave up their car, their cane, their wheelchair, and then their kitchen
    only to move to a hospital bed
whose pressure-sensitive mattress didn't prevent bed sores
who smiled despite dementia and dentures
who still celebrated Christmas and Thanksgiving and Easter and
    birthdays with cake and candles and presents like
    Frango Mints and Old Spice
who fell down so many times we lost count, making dents in the
    plaster walls that we spackled and painted, making dents
    in the car from driving
who could recite the Gettysburg Address, look you dead
    in the eye and say they are proud of you, then ask who planted bombs
    in their bed
who cried and shrieked about what they saw in the yellow wallpaper,
    then turned over and went to sleep for good
who got angry and made fists and accusations, full of grief
    and depression and fear and terminal anxiety
who sometimes thought of lonely gravestones with roses and crosses
    but as atheists turned their backs again and again against God

who learned to breathe all over again with oxygen machines
    before learning to let go of life
who once flew a B-47 and made a hole-in-one and whose demented wife
    was always leaving for Alaska very, very soon.

II

Schade! Isolation! Loneliness! Children weeping in the next room.
    Fathers wearing diapers. Prisoners of nursing homes!
Schade! The elderly man with heart disease and diabetes who just wants
    some cheese popcorn, even though he's on a restricted diet.
    Just give him some cheese popcorn!
I have seen Alzheimer's patients walk into *Nighthawks, Starry Night,*
    Sunflowers, Haystacks, The Yellow Room.
I have seen CNA students huddled in the corners of nursing home
    halls, dodging their duties, while minimum wage laborers wash
    residents' clothing and sometimes lose shirts or socks.
Schade to those who cannot walk without a cane, who cannot toilet
    without aid, who cannot eat without help, or defecate without a laxative.
Schade to experimental drugs for arthritis, and shots of Cortisone that
    leave shoulders and knees numb. *Schade* to addicting pain pills!
Schade to the wandering lost soul who forces her caretaker to chain
    the front door. The father who bravely walks across his cement garage
    floor! Who trips and hits his head on a car! The kind neighbor who rides
    in the ambulance with him all the way to the hospital, where he receives
    twenty-four different tests, an IV, and claims everything is fine, despite a
    rash that covers half his body.
The man shriveled up in a hospital bed eating crumbled vitamins in apple
    sauce!
The lady who needs a catheter for four years, and suffers chronic
    infections!
Schade to those who search for the Fountain of Youth! Who fly to Florida
    each year and collect social security and a pension, which is never enough.
Schade to demented patients who sign their last will and testament while
    half asleep, and place everything into the hands of a POA.

Schade when mothers can't swallow anymore, and food gets trapped in
   a lung, which leads to spastic breathing, to pneumonia, which leads
   to death.
Schade to the wheelchair-bound patient who rides in the PACE bus to
   adult daycare, that seems like a cruise on the Riviera, where he
   receives cupcakes, and does crafts, and participates in chair exercises,
   and physical therapy is like skiing down the Alps.
Ah, Mother, who smiled and comforted despite delirium and discomfort!
Ah, Father, with your crossed eye, hiccups, jaundiced skin and rash,
   who despite all this—can still express concern and salute your
   children.

III

Father, I'm with you in Plainfield, where you must feel very strange.
I'm with you in Plainfield, where your caretaker gives you a sponge bath,
   where you get to decide on fish or chicken for dinner,
   where you wave bye-bye each night to Vanna White.
I'm with you in Plainfield, where there are stains on your carpet,
   where a medicine chest lies aligned to your hospital bed,
   where you stare into a mirror and see your long dead father and
   brother.
I'm with you in Plainfield, where I hug and kiss you,
   for who knows when it will be our last?
I'm with you in Plainfield, where you wake up and try to throw yourself
   over the guard rails of your bed and walk out of your life.
I'm with you in Plainfield, and I don't blame you for trying to escape.
   In my dreams, you fly your B-47 across America and land outside my
   door, pick me up, and we take off into the starry night.

---

* *Der Schrei means "The Scream" in German. Schade! is German for "What a pity!"*

Acknowledgments

A special thank you to poet friends who spent time to carefully critique my manuscript, especially Wilda Morris, Ruan Wright, Robin Chapman and Christine Swanberg. I also want to thank all who believed in this project, including my publisher at Holy Cow! Press, Jim Perlman, and members of my weekly Friday writing group, Fereshteh Azad and Bakul Banerjee. My two sisters, Brenda Grossman and Becky McLaughlan, provided priceless support to me while I was going through the whole ordeal of caregiving, and my brother Bob observed my parents' decline from the front lines also. As always, my husband Bill was and still is my best teacher and critic.

This book, in a different version, was a finalist in the 2016 National Federation of State Poetry Societies (NFSPS) Stevens Manuscript Contest, and a semi-finalist in the 2015 and 2016 Concrete Wolf Louis Poetry Book Award competition.

Some poems published in this book first appeared in journals and anthologies, or won awards:

"*Der Schrei*" was published in *Origins Journal*. It won 3rd Place in the 2014 Poets & Patrons Chicagoland Contest, and was a semi-finalist in the 22nd Annual Gwendolyn Brooks Open Mic competition in Chicago.

"Sunsets" appeared in 2013 in *The Quotable*, and was nominated for a Pushcart Prize. It also won 3rd Honorable Mention, Laurel Crown Foundation Award, 2013 NFSPS Contest.

"At the Dentist" appeared in the Summer 2015 issue of *After Hours Magazine*.

"Bones" appeared in *Street Light Press.*

"Navigare Vivere Est" won 1st Honorable Mention in the 2012 Poets & Patrons Contest, Free Verse category.

"Just Three Words," "Your Last Chance," "Borders," "Taking Flight," "The Longest Good-Bye," "Coyote" and "Alzheimer's Dream" appeared in the chapbook *My Mother's Artwork.* "A Mother's Love" also appeared in the chapbook, and won 3rd Honorable Mention in the 2005 Poets & Patrons Chicagoland Contest.

"Becoming Erudite" was previously published in a different version in *Prairie Light Review* under the title, "Losing Control."

"Life's Melody" was published in *Exact Change Only.*

"Dangerous Driving" was published in the online journal *Voices on the Wind.*

"Gliding" won 1st place, League of Minnesota Award, 2015 NFSPS Contest, and was published in *Encore* in 2016; it won 2nd place in the 2014 Illinois State Poetry Society Contest, "Journey" category.

"Wandering" in a different version won 3rd Honorable Mention, Nebraska State Poetry Award, 2011 NFSPS Contest, and is forthcoming for publication in *Writers Tribe Review.*

"This Old Soldier" appeared in *The Popcorn Farm.*

"Crossing" won Wilda Morris's Poetry Challenge Contest for October, 2015, and was published on her blog.

"The Caregiver" appeared in *Lunch Ticket*, and is published in *Take Care: Tales, Tips and Love from Women Caregivers* (Braughler Books, 2017). It was nominated by *Lunch Ticket* for the 2016 Best of the Net.

"A Father's Invitation" won 3rd Honorable Mention in the 2015 Illinois State Poetry Society Contest, Formal Verse category. It appeared in the 2017 anthology, *Connoisseurs of Suffering* (University of Professors Press, 2017).

"Hospice" won 2nd Place in the 2015 Illinois State Poetry Society Contest, "Hope" category, and appeared in the anthology, *Take Care: Tales, Tips and Love from Women Caregivers*. "A Good Day" is also published in the same anthology.

"Ode to My Father's Nursing Home" won 3rd place in the 2016 Poets & Patrons Chicagoland Contest, Free Verse category, and won an honorable mention in the 2017 NFSPS Contest.

"Shut-Ins" appeared in *The Best of Kindness* anthology, Origami Poems Project, 2016.

"Skiing" won 1st place in the Free Verse category, 2017 Poets & Patrons Chicagoland Contest, and won an honorable mention in the 2017 NFSPS Contest.

"Exile" won 1st place in the Love category, 2017 Poets & Patrons Chicagoland Contest.

"Triptych in Color" won an Honorable Mention in the Chicago Arts category, 2017 Poets & Patrons Chicagoland Contest.

About the Author

Caroline Johnson observed both of her parents suffer crippling illnesses such as Multiple System Atrophy (MSA), Alzheimer's, and Rheumatoid Arthritis in the more than twelve years she spent as family caregiver. During that time she wrote poetry as a way to grieve and celebrate their life. This book is the culmination of that effort. She also has two poetry chapbooks, *My Mother's Artwork* and *Where the Street Ends*, and more than 70 poems in print. Her awards include winning the 2012 *Chicago Tribune's* Printers Row Poetry Contest, nominations for the Pushcart Prize and Best of the Net, and prizes in state and national competitions. A former English teacher, she works as an advisor for a Chicago area community college. One of her favorite activities in the past was watching James Bond movies with her father, who served in the U.S. Air Force as a bomber pilot during the Cold War in the 1950s as part of the Strategic Air Command (SAC).

For more information, please visit *www.caroline-johnson.com*